Nov 1 - 2001

To dear
darling Jen —
"At First babes
feed on the Mother's
bosom, but always on
her heart" Henry Ward
Beecher.

Love always, Bingo
Great

WG

Mothers Are Forever

Mothers Are Forever

Quotations Honoring the
Wisest Women We Know

Compiled and Edited by Criswell Freeman

WALNUT GROVE PRESS
Nashville, TN 37205

ISBN 1-887655-76-X

The ideas expressed in this book are not, in all cases, exact quotations, as some have been edited for clarity and brevity. In all cases, the author has attempted to maintain the speaker's original intent. In some cases, material for this book was obtained from secondary sources, primarily print media. While every effort was made to ensure the accuracy of these sources, the accuracy cannot be guaranteed. For additions, deletions, corrections or clarifications in future editions of this text, please write WALNUT GROVE PRESS.

Printed in the United States of America
Typesetting & Page Layout by Sue Gerdes
Editor for Walnut Grove Press: Alan Ross
6 7 8 9 10 •   01 02

ACKNOWLEDGMENTS
The author gratefully acknowledges the helpful support of Angela Freeman, Dick and Mary Freeman, Mary Susan Freeman and Jim Gallery.

For Mom

Table of Contents

Introduction

Motherhood, other claims to the contrary, is the world's oldest profession — and its most important. This little book celebrates the joys and responsibilities of the job.

Lin Yutang observed, "Of all the rights of women, the greatest is to be a mother." Yutang understood that a good mother does more than give birth; she shapes life.

The quotations herein remind us that a mother, as she raises her child, places her mark upon eternity. And we children are eternally grateful.

1

A Mother Is…

A mother is many things: She is the giver of life and love, the maker of house and home. She is chief cook and bottle washer, babysitter of last resort, provider, educator, doctor, disciplinarian, spiritual guide, counselor, health inspector, clothing consultant and taxi driver.

On the pages that follow, we consider various aspects of motherhood. It's a tough job, but someone has to do it… thank goodness for willing mothers.

Motherhood is the greatest privilege of life.

May Roper Coker

A mother is…
the holiest thing alive.

Samuel Taylor Coleridge

The woman who creates and sustains a home
is a creator second only to God.

Helen Hunt Jackson

The commonest fallacy among women is that
simply having children makes one a mother —
which is as absurd as believing that having
a piano makes one a musician.

Sydney J. Harris

Mothers are the most important actors
in the grand drama of human progress.

Elizabeth Cady Stanton

The mother is the unchartered servant
of the future.

Katherine Anthony

More than in any other human relationship,
overwhelmingly more, motherhood
means being instantly interruptible,
responsive, responsible.

Tillie Olsen

We bear the world, and we make it.
There was never a great man
who had not a great mother.

Olive Schreiner

Every mother is like Moses. She does not
enter the promised land. She prepares a world
she will not see.

Pope Paul VI

It's the mother who can cure her child's tears.

African Proverb

The God to whom little boys say their prayers
has a face very much like their mother's.

Sir James M. Barrie

Like mother, like daughter.

Old Saying

Her children arise up, and call her blessed.

Proverbs 31:28

Mother is the name for God on the lips and
in the hearts of little children.

William Makepeace Thackeray

Every mother thinks her child is beautiful.

Yiddish Proverb

A mother understands what her child
doesn't say.

Yiddish Proverb

All that I am, or hope
to be, I owe to my
angel mother.

Abraham Lincoln

What the mother sings to the cradle goes
all the way down to the coffin.

Henry Ward Beecher

The role of mother is probably the most
important career a woman can have.

Janet Mary Riley

A mother is not a person to lean on
but a person to make leaning unnecessary.

Dorothy Canfield Fisher

Who ran to help me when I fell,
     And would some pretty story tell,
     Or kiss the place to make it well?
     My mother.

Ann Taylor

Our mother interposes herself between us and
the world, protecting us from overwhelming
anxiety. We shall have no greater need
than this need for our mother.

Judith Viorst

Be thou then, O thou dear Mother,
    my atmosphere; my happier world.

Gerard Manley Hopkins

As a mother, my job is to take care of the possible and trust God with the impossible.

Ruth Bell Graham

Motherhood is the biggest on-the-job training program in existence today.

Erma Bombeck

Motherhood is more art than science.

Melinda Marshall

God could not be everywhere, so He made mothers.

Jewish Proverb

The best academy
is a mother's knee.

James Russell Lowell

An ounce of mother
is worth a ton of priest.

Spanish Proverb

2

Family

To belong to a happy family is among the richest blessings known to man. But this blessing is not gifted from above; it must be earned by parents and their children.

An old proverb reminds us, "When the family is together, the soul is at peace." The mother, as centerpiece of the household, helps hold the family together. But she, by herself, cannot produce a happy family. Family living is a team sport that requires cooperation from fathers, daughters, and sons.

Raising a family is more art than science, more guesswork than certainty. But one thing remains sure: When the family is together, mother is the officer of the peace. On the pages that follow, we consider an assortment of peace offerings.

The mother! She is what
keeps the family intact.
It is proved. A fact.

Anna F. Trevisan

The family — that dear octopus from whose
tentacles we never quite escape, nor,
in our inmost hearts, ever quite wish to.

Dodie Smith

A happy family is but an earlier heaven.

Sir John Bowring

A family is one of nature's masterpieces.

George Santayana

Call it a clan, call it a network, call it a tribe,
call it a family. Whatever you call it,
whoever you are, you need one.

Jane Howard

A family is the school of duties
        founded on love.

Felix Adler

A large family gives beauty to a house.

Indian Proverb

Family life! The United Nations is child's play
    compared to the tugs and splits and need
    to understand and forgive in any family.

May Sarton

A family is a unit composed not only
        of children, but of men, women,
an occasional animal, and the common cold.

Ogden Nash

A family is the we of me.

Carson McCullers

Nobody's family can hang out the sign
"Nothing the Matter Here."

Chinese Proverb

All happy families resemble one another;
every unhappy family is unhappy
in its own way.

Leo Tolstoy

A family is a court of justice
which never shuts down, for night or day.

Malcolm de Chazal

A family divided against itself
will perish together.

Indian Proverb

Bringing up a family should be an adventure
not an anxious discipline in which everybody
is constantly graded for performance.

Milton R. Sapirstein

Govern a family as you would cook
a small fish — very gently.

Chinese Proverb

What families have in common the world
around is that they are the place where people
learn who they are and how to be that way.

Jean Illsley Clarke

Healthy families are
      our greatest national resource.

Dolores Curran

Family jokes, though rightly cursed by strangers,
are the bond that keeps most families alive.

Stella Benson

You leave home to seek your fortune,
and when you get it, you go home and share it
      with your family.

Anita Baker

Heirlooms we don't have in our family.
      But stories we've got.

Rose Chernin

Whoever is ashamed of his family
will have no luck.

Yiddish Proverb

Comparison is a death knell to sibling harmony.

Elizabeth Fishel

Honor your father-in-law and mother-in-law,
for they are now your parents.

Yiddish Saying

I think we're seeing in working mothers
a change from "Thank God it's Friday"
to "Thank God it's Monday."

Ann Diehl

Spoil your husband, but don't spoil your children. That's my philosophy.

Louise Sevier Giddings Currey
1961 Mother of the Year

A man should never
hesitate to alleviate a
father's or mother's grief,
even at the risk of his life.

Buddhist Saying

3

Love

Good mothers come in a wide range of shapes, sizes, colors, temperaments and nationalities; but they all share a singular trait: maternal love. Sometimes, that devotion is tested to the limits. Even well-intended children behave, from time to time, in ways that only a mother could love.

The following quotations pay tribute to the common denominator of every magnificent mom: a heart big enough to love us kids   in spite of ourselves.

Love stretches your heart
and makes you big inside.

Margaret Walker

Love is a great beautifier.

Louisa May Alcott

Love is the key to every good.

Doris Lessing

The giving of love is an education in itself.

Eleanor Roosevelt

Love is, above all, the gift of oneself.

Jean Anouilh

Love yourself first.

Lucille Ball

Love is a multiplication.

Marjory Stoneman Douglas

Love is patient; love is kind and envies no one.
Love is never boastful, nor conceited, nor rude;
never selfish, not quick to take offense.

I Corinthians 13:4-5

Love is the subtlest force in the world.

Mohandas Gandhi

A successful marriage
requires falling in love
many times, always with
the same person.

Mignon McLaughlin

It takes a long time
to be *really* married.

Ruby Dee

There is nothing more lovely in life than
the union of two people whose love for one
another has grown through the years from the
small acorn of passion to a great-rooted tree.

Vita Sackville-West

A good marriage is one which allows
for change and growth in the individuals
and in the way they express their love.

Pearl Buck

Love does not consist in gazing at each other
but in looking outward together
in the same direction.

Antoine de Saint Exupéry

Nothing in life is as good as the marriage of
true minds between man and woman. As good?
It is life itself.

Pearl Buck

Be completely humble and gentle; be patient
bearing with one another in love.

Ephesians 4:2

And now abideth faith, hope, love,
these three; but the greatest of these is love.

I Corinthians 13:13

Maternal love: a miraculous substance
which God multiplies as he divides it.

Victor Hugo

Yet have I looked into my mother's eyes and
seen the light that never was on sea or land,
the light of love, pure love and true,
and on that love I bet my life.

G. A. Studdert Kennedy

You don't have to deserve your mother's love.
You have to deserve your father's.

Robert Frost

A mother's love! O holy,
boundless thing!
Fountain whose waters
never cease to spring.

Marguerite Blessington

If you love only those who love you,
what reward can you expect?

Matthew 5:46

It is impossible for any woman to love
her children twenty-four hours a day.

Milton R. Sapirstein

Everything in life that we really accept
undergoes a change; so suffering must
become love. That is the mystery.

Katherine Mansfield

Life is like a blanket too short.
You pull it up and your toes rebel, you yank it
down and shivers meander about your shoulders;
but cheerful folks manage to draw their knees up
and pass a comfortable night.

Marion Howard

Life is the flower of which love is the honey.

Victor Hugo

Whoever loves true love will love true life.

Elizabeth Barrett Browning

The fragrance always remains in the hand
that gives the rose.

Heda Bejar

Youth fades; love droops;
the leaves of friendship fall.
A mother's secret love outlives them all.

Oliver Wendell Holmes, Sr.

Love dies only when growth stops.

Leo Buscaglia

It's not love's going that hurts my days,
But that it went in little ways.

Edna St. Vincent Millay

There is only one terminal
dignity — love.

Helen Hayes

When the evening of this
life comes, we shall be
judged on love.

St. John of the Cross

A single night of universal love could save everything.

Roland Giguère

4

The Home

The noted jurist Oliver Wendell Holmes, Jr. once observed, "Anywhere we love is home." All who have experienced the warmth of a love-filled household can second that emotion.

Home is not simply a place; it is a state of mind, built as much with love as with brick and mortar. The size of a house is relatively unimportant; the collective size of the hearts that dwell inside is all-important.

On the pages that follow, notable men and women share their blueprints for the greatest structure known to mankind: a happy home.

Love can make any place
agreeable.

Old Saying

Make yourself happy
where you are adored.

Isabella de' Medici Orsini

Home — that blessed word which opens
to the human heart the most perfect
glimpse of Heaven.

Lydia M. Child

Make two homes for thyself:
one actual home and another spiritual home
which thou art to carry with thee always.

St. Catherine of Siena

Home is any four walls that enclose
the right person.

Helen Rowland

A good laugh is sunshine in a house.

William Makepeace Thackeray

It takes a heap of lovin' in a house to make it
a home.

Edgar A. Guest

Lonely? Dull? Not as long as I can have
our friends gather around our fireplace
or about our stone table for a picnic
under the maples in the summer.

Nancy Ford Cones

A house may draw visitors, but it is the
possessor alone that can detain them.

Charles Caleb Colton

The ornament of a house is the friends
who frequent it.

Ralph Waldo Emerson

We need not power or splendor;
    Wide hall or lordly dome;
    The good, the true, the tender,
    These form the wealth of home.

Sarah Josepha Hale

The ideal of happiness has always taken
material form in the house, whether cottage or
castle. It stands for permanence and separation
from the world.

Simone de Beauvoir

A house is no home unless it contains food
and fire for the mind as well as for the body.

Margaret Fuller

Radio, sewing machine, book ends, ironing
board and that great piano lamp — peace,
that's what I like.

Eudora Welty

Our only chance for survival lies in creating
our own little islands of sanity and order,
in making little havens of our homes.

Sue Kaufman

There is nothing like staying at home
for real comfort.

Jane Austen

Home is not where you live
but where they understand you.

Christian Morgenstern

Home is a restaurant which never closes.

Anonymous

Now, as always, the most automated appliance in a household is the mother.

Beverly Jones

Instant availability without continuous presence
is probably the best role a mother can play.

Lotte Bailyn

God forbid that I should will any
to do that in my house which
I would not willingly do myself.

Margaret Clitherow

It is a proud moment in a woman's life to reign
supreme within four walls; to be the one to
whom all questions of domestic pleasure and
economy are referred.

Elizabeth Cady Stanton

Housekeeping is no joke.

Louisa May Alcott

Cleaning your house
        while your kids are still growing
            is like shoveling the walk
                before it stops snowing.

Phyllis Diller

They that think much and are not willing to do
such base things as housework have little regard
of well-doing or knowledge of themselves.

Margaret Clitherow

To the old saying that "man built the house,
but woman made it a home" might be added
the modern supplement that woman accepted
cooking as a chore but man has made of it
a recreation.

Emily Post

It is certainly true that housekeeping cares
bring with them a thousand
endearing compensations.

Marceline Desbordes-Valmore

It is the personality of the mistress that
the house expresses. Men are forever guests
in our homes, no matter how much happiness
they may find there.

Elsie De Wolfe

A man is *so* in the way
in the house!

Elizabeth Gaskell

Better a hundred enemies outside the house
than one inside.

Arabian Proverb

Charity too often not only begins
but ends at home.

Anonymous

Frugality without creativity is deprivation.

Amy Dacyczyn

Home is where the mortgage is.

Anonymous

A home is the place of
last resort, open all night.

Ambrose Bierce

Home wasn't built in a day.

Jane Ace

5

Children

Were it not for kids, motherhood would be a breeze. But children, of course, are the singular requirement of a mother's job description. Raising a family requires an endless supply of love, patience, understanding and work. But every mother knows that the potential payoff is worth the effort.

Henry Ward Beecher proclaimed, "Children are the hands by which we take hold of heaven." A mother, by taking firm hold of her child's hand, creates a little piece of heaven on earth. The following quotations celebrate the joy of creation.

Of all the haunting
moments of motherhood,
few rank with hearing your
own words come out of
your daughter's mouth.

Victoria Secunda

A child is the greatest
poem ever known.

Christopher Morley

A baby is God's opinion that life should go on.
Carl Sandburg

A child is a beam of sunlight
from the Infinite and Eternal.
Lyman Abbott

No animal is so inexhaustible
as an excited infant.
Amy Leslie

A child is someone who stands
halfway between an adult and a TV set.
Anonymous

All children are artists, and it is an indictment
of our culture that so many of them lose their
creativity, their unfettered imaginations,
as they grow older.

Madeleine L'Engle

A child's attitude toward everything
is an artist's attitude.

Willa Cather

A child is a curly, dimpled lunatic.

Ralph Waldo Emerson

Insanity is hereditary: you can get it
from your children.

Sam Levenson

No one has yet fully realized the wealth
of sympathy, kindness and generosity hidden
in the soul of a child.

Emma Goldman

Wherever children are learning,
there dwells the Divine Presence.

Old Saying

A son and his mother are godly.

Rochelle Owens

The voice of parents is the voice of gods,
for to their children, they are heaven's lieutenants.

William Shakespeare

Even when freshly washed and relieved of all
obvious confections, children tend to be sticky.

Fran Lebowitz

For the parents of a Little Leaguer,
a baseball game is simply a nervous breakdown
into innings.

Earl Wilson

Adorable children are considered to be the
general property of the human race.
Rude children belong to their mothers.

Judith Martin

Parents of young children should realize that
few people will find their children
as enchanting as they do.

Barbara Walters

A mother understands what a child
does not say.

Old Saying

Even a child is known by its deeds.

Old Saying

Sometimes when I look at all my children, I say to myself, "Lillian, you should have stayed a virgin."

Lillian Carter

Never allow your child to call you by your
first name. He hasn't known you long enough.

Fran Lebowitz

No matter how old a mother is,
   she watches her middle-aged children
      for signs of improvement.

Florida Scott-Maxwell

Ask your child what he wants for dinner
         only if he's buying.

Fran Lebowitz

One hour with a child is like a ten-mile run.

Joan Benoit Samuelson

I looked on raising children not only as a work
of love and duty but as a profession that
demanded the best that I could bring to it.

Rose Kennedy

Children are likely to live up to
what you believe of them.

Lady Bird Johnson

What we desire our children to become,
we must endeavor to be before them.

Andrew Combe

What feeling is so nice as a child's hand
in yours? So small, so soft and warm, like a
kitten huddling in the shelter of your clasp.

Marjorie Holmes

What good mothers and fathers instinctively
feel like doing for their babies
is usually best after all.

Benjamin Spock

The character and history of each child may
be a new and poetic experience to the parent,
if he will let it.

Margaret Fuller

All children alarm their parents,
if only because you are forever expecting
to encounter yourself.

Gore Vidal

Parents learn a lot from their children
about coping with life.

Muriel Spark

Love your children with all your hearts,
love them enough to discipline them
before it is too late.

Lavina Christensen Fugal

At every step the child should be allowed
to meet the real experiences of life; the thorns
should never be plucked from their roses.

Ellen Key

It is not a bad thing that children should
occasionally, and politely, put parents
in their place.

Colette

Loving a child doesn't mean giving in to all
his whims; to love him is to bring out the best in
him, to teach him to love what is difficult.

Nadia Boulanger

It is better to keep children to their duty
by a sense of honor and by kindness than by fear.

Terence

The hearts of small children
are delicate organs.

Carson McCullers

The mother's heart is the child's schoolroom.

Henry Ward Beecher

The debt of gratitude we owe our mother
and father goes forward, not backward.
What we owe our parents is the bill
presented to us by our children.

Nancy Friday

Our children are not going to be just *our*
children — they are going to be other people's
husbands and wives and the parents
of our grandchildren.

Mary S. Calderone

Let every father and mother understand
that when their child is three years old,
they have done more than half of all
they will ever do for its character.

Horace Bushnell

We are together, my child and I, mother and
child, yes, but *sisters* really, against whatever
denies us all that we are.

Alice Walker

When a child enters the world through you,
it alters everything.

Jane Fonda

My mama raised me right.

Elvis Presley

Children have more need of models
than critics.

Joseph Joubert

Parents must get across the idea that
"I love you always, but sometimes I do not love
your behavior."

Amy Vanderbilt

The best things you can give children,
next to good habits, are good memories.

Sydney J. Harris

It takes courage to let our children go,
but we are trustees and stewards and have to
hand them back to life — to God.
We have to love them and lose them.

Alfred Torrie

Zoroaster tells us that children are a bridge joining this earth to a heavenly paradise, filled with fresh springs and blooming gardens.

Lydia M. Child

A child's tears move the heavens themselves.

Old Saying

If you want a baby, have a new one. Don't baby the old one.

Jessamyn West

Before I had children,
I held on to the illusion
that there was order
in the universe.

Susan Lapinski

6

Happiness

Her child's happiness is a mother's ambition. But as time passes and adulthood approaches, happiness becomes the responsibility of the child, not the parent. No one, not even a loving mother, can make a gift of contentment. Each of us must earn it for ourselves.

While unable to bestow peace of mind, a thoughtful mother *can* show her child that peace of mind is possible. She does so by example not decree.

On the pages that follow, notable men and women share practical prescriptions for happiness. Every mother can teach these lessons *and* live them ... and should.

The right to happiness
is fundamental.

Anna Pavlova

Take time each day to do something silly.
Philipa Walker

I had a pleasant time with my mind,
for it was happy.
Louisa May Alcott

All times are beautiful for those who maintain
joy within themselves.
Rosalia Castro

Until you make peace with who you are,
you'll never be content with what you have.
Doris Mortman

Happiness is not a goal; it is a by-product.
Eleanor Roosevelt

Happiness is a by-product of an effort
to make someone else happy.
Gretta Palmer

Happiness is nothing but everyday living
seen through a veil.
Zora Neale Hurston

Growth itself contains the germ of happiness.
Pearl Buck

Happiness walks on busy feet.

Kitte Turmell

Change is an easy panacea. It takes character to stay in one place and be happy there.
Elizabeth Clarke Dunn

It isn't the great big pleasures that count the most; it's making a great deal out of the little ones.
Jean Webster

I have the greatest of all riches: that of not desiring them.
Eleonora Duse

Be content with such things as ye have.
Hebrews 13:5

Happiness is a life spent learning,
earning and yearning.

Lillian Gish

One must never look for happiness.
One meets it by the way.

Isabelle Eberhardt

It is not easy to find happiness in ourselves,
and it is not possible to find it elsewhere.

Agnes Repplier

True happiness is not attained through
self-gratification but through fidelity
to a worthy cause.

Helen Keller

One of the luckiest
things that can happen
to you in life is, I think,
to have a happy childhood.

Agatha Christie

Talk happiness. The world is sad enough
without your woe.

Ella Wheeler Wilcox

Happiness is not a matter of events;
it depends upon the tides of the minds.

Alice Meynell

Be happy. It's one way of being wise.

Colette

To live and let live without clamor for
  distinction or recognition; to wait on divine
Love; to write truth first on the tablet of one's
own heart — this is the sanity and perfection
  of living and my human ideal.

Mary Baker Eddy

No one's happiness but my own
  is in my power to achieve or to destroy.

Ayn Rand

New happiness too must be learned to bear.

Marie von Ebner-Eschenbach

Birds sing after a storm;
why shouldn't people
feel as free to delight in
whatever remains to them?

Rose Kennedy

If only we'd stop trying to be happy, we'd have a pretty good time.

Edith Wharton

7

Faith

Life is a grand adventure made great by faith. Enduring faith is first experienced at mother's knee. There, the child learns to trust not only in the parent but also the world.

If *you're* looking for a message to share with future generations, preach the gospel of faith: faith in the future, faith in one's fellow man, and faith in the Hand that shapes eternity. No message is more important.

You're not free until
you've been made captive
by supreme belief.

Marianne Moore

Without faith, nothing
is possible. With it,
nothing is impossible.

Mary McLeod Bethune

Faith is to believe in something not yet proved and to underwrite it with our lives. It is the only way we can leave the future open.

Lillian Smith

Faith is the assertion of a possibility against all probabilities.

Ethelbert Stauffer

Faith is putting all your eggs in God's basket, then counting your blessings before they hatch.

Ramona C. Carroll

Faith is the key to fit the door of hope,
but there is no power anywhere like love
for turning it.

Elaine Emans

Faith is the substance of things hoped for,
the evidence of things not seen.

Hebrews: 11:1

Faith is the subtle chain which binds us
to the infinite.

Elizabeth Oakes Smith

So with faith, if it does
not lead to action,
it is in itself
a lifeless thing.

James 2:17

Faith is the little night-light that burns in a sick-room. As long as it is there, the obscurity is not complete. We turn towards it and await the daylight.

Abbe Huvelin

Faith sees the invisible, believes the incredible
and receives the impossible.

Unknown

It is by believing in roses that one brings
them to bloom.

French Proverb

Faith is the sturdiest of the virtues.
It is the virtue of the storm, just as happiness
is the virtue of sunshine.

Ruth Benedict

I was always looking outside myself
for strength and confidence, but it comes
from within. It was there all the time.

Anna Freud

Hope deferred maketh the heart sick.

Proverbs 13:12

To eat bread without hope is still slowly
to starve to death.

Pearl Buck

Faith is the flip side of fear.

Susan Taylor

Faith is the only known cure for fear.

Lena K. Sadler

Faith is like a radar that sees through the fog —
the reality of things at a distance that the
human eye cannot see.

Corrie Ten Boom

To have faith where you cannot see; to be
willing to work on in the dark; to be conscious
of the fact that there are better things on the way;
this is success.

Katherine Logan

Build in darkness if you have faith.
When the light returns, you have made
of yourself a fortress which is impregnable.

Olga Rosmanith

If life is a comedy to those who think and a tragedy to those who feel, it is a victory to those who believe.

Unknown

The future belongs to those who believe in the beauty of their dreams.

Eleanor Roosevelt

8

Life

First mothers give life, then they teach it. On the following pages, we consider a few lessons that any mother would be proud to call her own.

There is something all life
has in common, and
when I know what it is,
I shall know myself.

Jean Craighead George

If you let yourself be absorbed completely,
if you surrender completely to the moments
as they pass, you live more richly.

Anne Morrow Lindbergh

Each day, and the living of it, has to be
a conscious creation in which discipline
and order are relieved with some play
and pure foolishness.

May Sarton

Life is either a daring adventure or nothing.
To keep our faces toward change and behave
like free spirits in the presence of fate is
strength undefeatable.

Helen Keller

To live fully, outwardly and inwardly,
not to ignore external reality for the sake of the
inner life, or the reverse — that's quite a task.

Etty Hillesum

We're all in this together — by ourselves.

Lily Tomlin

If you wish to live, you must first attend
your own funeral.

Katherine Mansfield

They are committing murder who merely live.

May Sarton

I am one of those people who just can't help
getting a kick out of life — even when it's
a kick in the teeth.

Polly Adler

To live exhilaratingly in and for the moment
is deadly serious work, fun of the most
exhausting sort.

Barbara Grizzuti Harrison

How we spend our days is, of course,
how we spend our lives.

Annie Dillard

Life begets life. Energy creates energy. It is
by spending oneself that one becomes rich.

Sarah Bernhardt

She seems to have had the ability to stand
firmly on the rock of her past, while living
completely and unregretfully in the present.

Madeleine L'Engle

I love my past. I love my present. I'm not
ashamed of what I've had, and I'm not sad
because I have it no longer.

Colette

I have learned to live each day as it comes and
not to borrow trouble by dreading tomorrow.
It is the dark menace of the future
that makes cowards of us all.

Dorothy Dix

All life is pattern —
but we can't always see
the pattern when
we're part of it.

Belva Plain

No one grows old by living,
only by losing interest in living.

Marie Beynon Ray

Yesterday is a cancelled check; tomorrow
is a promissory note; today is the only cash
you have — so spend it wisely.

Kay Lyons

Anyone who limits her vision to memories
of yesterday is already dead.

Lily Langtry

The past is finished. There is nothing to be
gained by going over it. Whatever it gave us in
the experiences it brought us was something
we had to know.

Rebecca Beard

Living is a form of not being sure. We guess. We may be wrong, but we take leap after leap in the dark.

Agnes de Mille

Mistakes are part of the dues one pays for a full life.

Sophia Loren

Remorse is the poison of life.

Charlotte Brontë

Life is meant to be lived, and curiosity must be kept alive. One must never, for whatever reason, turn his back on life.

Eleanor Roosevelt

Life is raw material. We are artisans.

Cathy Better

Life is what we make it. Always has been. Always will be.

Grandma Moses

Life has got to be lived — that's all there is to it.

Eleanor Roosevelt

Learn to drink the cup of life as it comes.

Agnes Turnbull

You don't get to choose how you're going to die,
or when. You can only decide
how you're going to live. Now!

Joan Baez

It's only when we truly know and understand
that we have a limited time on earth — that we
have no way of knowing when our time is up —
that we will begin to live each day to the fullest,
as if it were the only one we had.

Elisabeth Kübler-Ross

I gave my life to learning how to live. Now that
I have organized it all, it's just about over.

Sandra Hochman

I don't want to get to the end of my life
and find that I lived just the length of it.
I want to have lived the width of it as well.

Diane Ackerman

God, give me work till
my life shall end and life
till my work is done.

Winifred Holtby

9

Memories of Mom

Memories are precious, but memories of mom are perhaps the most precious of all. In this chapter, notable men and women share recollections of memorable mothers. Enjoy!

Mama gave us the role
model of someone who
knew how to juggle.
She was always there,
and yet she was always
working. We thought she
was the most beautiful
woman alive.

Cokie Roberts

Nothing is as precious
as my mama's memory.

Dolly Parton

My parents encouraged me to read and think.

Gwendolyn Brooks

Someday this girl will be the first lady
of something.

Jackie Joyner-Kersee's grandmother

My dad ended up selling vacuum cleaners,
and my mom got a job as a secretary.
They never got rich, and they never got famous,
but they showed me that you do things
for a purpose.

Julia Roberts

We didn't know how poor we were.
We were rich as a family.

Florence Griffith Joyner

The household was a full-time occupation.
I have one of the best mothers anyone could have.

Arnold Schwarzenegger

My mother is as tough as nails; a great
mother and a great woman, very independent.
She's constantly challenging herself. She has told
me that much has been given to me,
and therefore I should do something with it.

Maria Shriver

I had a wonderful, happy childhood.
I think my parents liked to inspire creativity
and productivity in their children.
Our happiness was important to them.

John Travolta

I think maybe comedy was part of my way
of connecting with my mother. I'd make
Mommy laugh and everything was OK.
That's where it started.

Robin Williams

My parents wanted to make sure that if we had a talent, we got the chance to develop it.

Alison Krauss

My father was on the road a great deal, and my mother ran the family. She believed in discipline. There was none of that Hollywood scene of the star's spoiled kids.

Natalie Cole

My mother worked at home as a seamstress. She would get angry if she was given a bad dress to work on. Subliminally, that stuck. I don't want to sing a song unless it's great.

Tony Bennett

My mother was a great storyteller,
a very free spirit who believed in creativity and
freedom of expression.

Anne Rice

My mother taught me
how to be inquisitive.

Heloise

My mother was also my best friend.
She left me with a rich endowment
of ideas and memories.

Faith Ringgold

The big factor in my life, in terms of my career, has always been my mother. She taught me that you have to watch out for the opportunities and not be afraid to take risks.

Lesley Stahl

My signature appears on $60 billion of U.S. currency. More importantly, however, is the signature that appears on my life — the strong, proud, assertive handwriting of a loving mother and father.

Katherine D. Ortega, Treasurer of the United States

It used to get to me when Mama, who is my biggest critic, was in the audience. But now that I'm a mama myself, I realize that she loves me regardless of how I do.

Reba McEntire

She was always
my best girl.

Elvis Presley

My mother was all mother.

Ella Fitzgerald

10

Motherly Advice

Few things in life are more useful than motherly advice. But the supply of this advice vastly outpaces the demand. Children seem destined to make their own mistakes despite parental preachments or maternal mandates. Each generation, it appears, must learn anew the lessons of the last.

The Talmud reminds us that "He who is best taught first learned from his mother." In this chapter, we consider tried-and-true motherly advice that is often taught and sometimes learned. All of us, mothers and children alike, can benefit from a refresher course.

If you always do what interests you, at least one person will be pleased.

Mother's Advice to Katherine Hepburn

My mother said to me, "If you become
a soldier, you'll be a general; if you become
a monk, you'll end up as the pope." Instead,
I became a painter and wound up as Picasso.

Pablo Picasso

She'd always say to me, "Don't think that
your looks are going to help in the long run,
because you'll be pretty today and someone
else will be prettier tomorrow. Make sure you
improve your brain, because that will make you
interesting."

Maria Shriver

She taught me to see beauty in all things
around me; that inside each thing a spirit lived,
that it was vital, too, regardless of whether it
was only a leaf or a blade of grass,
and by recognizing its life and beauty,
I was accepting God.

Maria Campbell

Fill what's empty.
Empty what's full.
And scratch where it itches.

Alice Roosevelt Longworth

It is not fair to ask
of others what you are not
willing to do yourself.

Eleanor Roosevelt

In youth we learn. In age we understand.

Marie von Ebner-Eschenbach

Nothing in life is to be feared.
It is only to be understood.

Marie Curie

Keep the other person's well-being in mind
when you feel an attack of soul-purging truth
coming on.

Betty White

People who fight fire with fire
end up with ashes.

Abigail Van Buren

Kind words can be short and easy to speak
but their echoes are truly endless.

Mother Teresa

If you judge people, you have no time
to love them.

Mother Teresa

It is by forgiving that one is forgiven.

Mother Teresa

You can't fake listening.

Raquel Welch

A mediocre idea that generates enthusiasm
will go farther than a great idea
that inspires no one.

Mary Kay Ash

Time wounds all heels.

Jane Ace

11

Observations About Mothers, Gardens and Other Gifts from God

We conclude with a potpourri of observations about motherhood. In Mom we trust … forever.

Never make fun of religion, race or mothers.

Mack Sennett

I never thought that you should be rewarded
for the greatest privilege of life.

May Roper Coker, 1958 Mother of the Year

As a mother I have served longer
than I expected.

Carol Emshwiller

The warmest bed of all is Mother's.

Old Saying

Five out of my five kids are too good
to be true, thanks to their mother.
She is a world-class mother.

Ross Perot

I wanted to make music
my mother would listen to.

Will Smith

In search of my mother's garden, I found my own.

Alice Walker

No man is poor who has
a Godly mother.

Abraham Lincoln

There are no shortcuts to any place
worth going.

Beverly Sills

To know how to do something well
is to enjoy it.

Pearl Buck

Service is the rent that you pay for room
on this earth.

Shirley Chisholm

What we are is God's gift to us.
What we become is our gift to God.

Eleanor Powell

Are anybody's parents typical?

Madeleine L'Engle

I know how to do anything — I'm a mom.

Roseanne Barr

Sources

About the Author

Criswell Freeman is a Doctor of Clinical Psychology living in Nashville, Tennessee. He is the author of *When Life Throws You a Curveball, Hit It* and numerous books in the Wisdom Series published by WALNUT GROVE PRESS.

Dr. Freeman's Wisdom Books chronicle memorable quotations in an easy-to-read style. The series provides inspiring, thoughtful and humorous messages from entertainers, athletes, scientists, politicians, clerics, writers and renegades, with each title focusing on a particular region or area of special interest. Combining his passion for quotations with extensive training in psychology, Freeman revisits timeless themes such as perseverance, courage, love, forgiveness and faith.

Dr. Freeman is also the host of *Wisdom Made in America*, a nationally syndicated radio program.

The Wisdom Series
by Dr. Criswell Freeman

Regional Titles

Wisdom Made in America	ISBN 1-887655-07-7
The Book of Southern Wisdom	ISBN 0-9640955-3-X
The Wisdom of the Midwest	ISBN 1-887655-17-4
The Wisdom of the West	ISBN 1-887655-31-X
The Book of Texas Wisdom	ISBN 0-9640955-8-0
The Book of Florida Wisdom	ISBN 0-9640955-9-9
The Book of California Wisdom	ISBN 1-887655-14-X
The Book of New York Wisdom	ISBN 1-887655-16-6
The Book of New England Wisdom	ISBN 1-887655-15-8

Sports Titles

The Golfer's Book of Wisdom	ISBN 0-9640955-6-4
The Putter Principle	ISBN 1-887655-39-5
The Golfer's Guide to Life	ISBN 1-887655-38-7
The Wisdom of Women's Golf	ISBN 1-887655-82-4
The Book of Football Wisdom	ISBN 1-887655-18-2
The Wisdom of Southern Football	ISBN 0-9640955-7-2
The Book of Stock Car Wisdom	ISBN 1-887655-12-3
The Wisdom of Old-Time Baseball	ISBN 1-887655-08-5
The Book of Basketball Wisdom	ISBN 1-887655-32-8
The Fisherman's Guide to Life	ISBN 1-887655-30-1
The Tennis Lover's Guide to Life	ISBN 1-887655-36-0

Special People Titles

Mothers Are Forever	ISBN 1-887655-76-X
Fathers Are Forever	ISBN 1-887655-77-8
Friends Are Forever	ISBN 1-887655-78-6
The Teacher's Book of Wisdom	ISBN 1-887655-80-8
The Graduate's Book of Wisdom	ISBN 1-887655-81-6
The Guide to Better Birthdays	ISBN 1-887655-35-2
Get Well Soon...If Not Sooner	ISBN 1-887655-79-4
The Wisdom of the Heart	ISBN 1-887655-34-4

Special Interest Titles

The Book of Country Music Wisdom	ISBN 0-9640955-1-3
Old-Time Country Wisdom	ISBN 1-887655-26-3
The Wisdom of Old-Time Television	ISBN 1-887655-64-6
The Book of Cowboy Wisdom	ISBN 1-887655-41-7
The Gardener's Guide to Life	ISBN 1-887655-40-9
The Salesman's Book of Wisdom	ISBN 1-887655-83-2
Minutes from the Great Women's Coffee Club (by Angela Beasley)	ISBN 1-887655-33-6